This Is What I Want to Be

Artist

Heather Miller

Heinemann Library

Chicago, Illinois

© 2003 Heinemann Library
a division of Reed Elsevier Inc.
Chicago, Illinois

Customer Service 888-454-2279
Visit our website at www.heinemannlibrary.com

Designed by Sue Emerson, Heineman Library; Page layout by Que-Net Media
Printed and bound in the United States by Lake Book Manufacturing, Inc.
Photo research by Alan Gottlieb

07 06 05 04 03
10 9 8 7 6 5 4 3 2 1

Library of Congress Cataloging-in-Publication Data
Miller, Heather.
    Artist / Heather Miller.
        v. cm. – (This is what I want to be)
Includes index.
Contents: What do artists do? – What is an artist's day like? – What tools do artists use? – Where do artists work? – Do artists work in other places? – When do artists work? – What kinds of artists are there? – Are there other kinds of artists? – How do people become artists?
    ISBN 1-4034-0913-7 (HC), 1-4034-3606-1 (Pbk.)
    1. Artists–Vocational guidance–Juvenile literature. [1. Artists. 2. Occupations.] I. Title.
    N8350 .M48 2003

                                    2002010292

Acknowledgments
The author and publishers are grateful to the following for permission to reproduce copyright material:
p. 4 Robert Holmes/Corbis; pp. 5, 7 Patrick Ward/Corbis; p. 6 Raymond Gehman/Corbis; p. 8 Rafael Macia/Photo Researchers, Inc.; p. 9L Peter Beck/Corbis; p. 9R Stewart Cohen/Stone/Getty Images; p. 10 Steve Frame/Stock Boston; p. 11 Jeffry W. Myers/Corbis; p. 12 Heinemann Library; p. 13 Jose Luis Pelaez, Inc./Corbis; p. 14 Royalty-Free/Corbis; p. 15 Lonnie Duka/Index Stock; p. 16 Brett Patterson/Corbis; p. 17 Jim Schwabel/Index Stock; p. 18 Will & Deni McIntyre/Photo Researchers, Inc.; p. 19 Mug Shots/Corbis; p. 20 Richard Pasley/Stock Boston; p. 21 David Butow/Corbis Saba; pp. 22, 24 PhotoDisc; p. 23 (row 1, L-R) Larry S. Voigt, Mug Shots/Corbis, Rafael Macia/Photo Researchers, Inc., PhotoDisc; (row 2, L-R) Will & Deni McIntyre/Photo Researchers, Inc., Mug Shots/Corbis, Steven Frame, Peter Beck/Corbis; (row 3, L-R) Heinemann Library, Will & Deni McIntyre/Photo Researchers, Inc., James L. Amos/Corbis, Heinemann Library; (row 4, L-R) Jeffry W. Myers/Corbis, Stewart Cohen/Stone/Getty Images, Ralph A. Clevenger/Corbis; back cover (L-R) Larry S. Voigt, Steven Frame

Cover photograph by Kevin Fleming/Corbis

Every effort has been made to contact copyright holders of any material reproduced in this book. Any omissions will be rectified in subsequent printings if notice is given to the publisher.

Special thanks to our advisory panel for their help in the preparation of this book:
Alice Bethke, Library Consultant
Palo Alto, CA

Eileen Day, Preschool Teacher
Chicago, IL

Kathleen Gilbert,
Second Grade Teacher
Round Rock, TX

Sandra Gilbert,
Library Media Specialist
Fiest Elementary School
Houston, TX

Jan Gobeille, Kindergarten Teacher
Garfield Elementary
Oakland, CA

Angela Leeper,
Educational Consultant
North Carolina Department
of Public Instruction
Wake Forest, NC

Some words are shown in bold, **like this.**
You can find them in the picture glossary on page 23.

Contents

What Do Artists Do?

Artists are people who make things.

They show feelings and ideas
with art.

Some artists sell their work.

Other artists make art just for fun.

What Is an Artist's Day Like?

Some artists spend their day in a **studio**.

They can work on many projects at a time.

Artists think of ideas for
new projects.

They may draw their ideas
on paper.

What Tools Do Artists Use?

Artists mix paints on a **palette**.

They spread paint with **brushes**.

chisel

hammer

knives

sponge

Some artists carve stone with **hammers** and **chisels**.

Others shape **clay** with **knives** and **sponges**.

9

Where Do Artists Work?

Some artists have **studios** in their homes.

Others work in buildings away from home.

Some artists work outdoors.

These artists are making a **mural**.

Do Artists Work in Other Places?

Artists can work at book companies.

They add pictures to books!

Other artists work in schools.

They teach people about art.

When Do Artists Work?

Artists can work at any time.

Some artists like to work in the morning.

Others work late at night.

Artists may work on one project for many days.

What Kinds of Artists Are There?

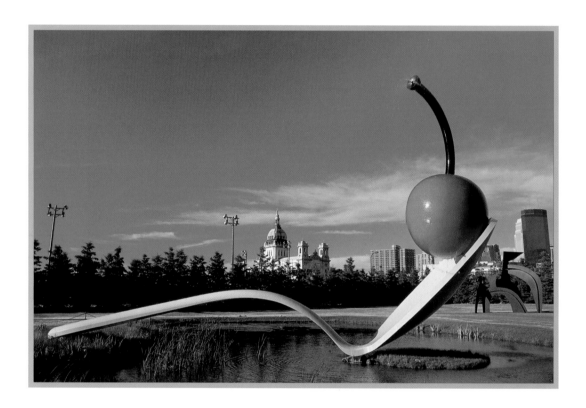

Sculptors make things with **wood**, metal, or **clay**.

Their art is called sculpture.

Painters make pictures with paint.

They paint people or things.

Are There Other Kinds of Artists?

Photographers are artists.

They take pictures of things with **cameras**.

This **glassblower** is an artist.

He is shaping hot glass into a **vase**.

How Do People Become Artists?

People go to art school.

They practice many kinds of art.

Artists learn from each other.

They try to find new ways to make art.

Quiz

Do you remember what these things are called?

Look for the answers on page 24.

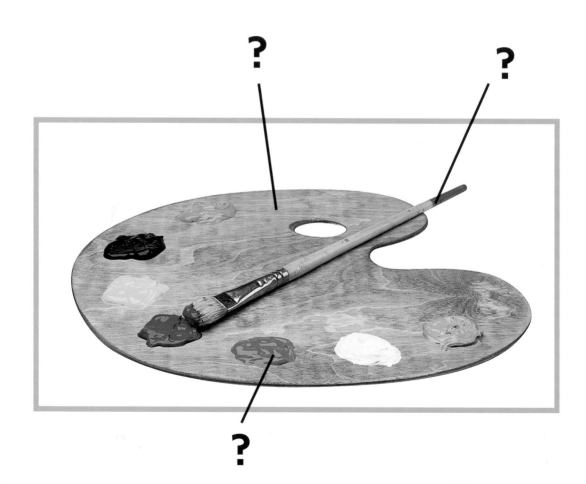

Picture Glossary

brushes
page 8

glassblower
page 19

painter
page 17

sponge
page 9

camera
page 18

hammer
page 9

palette
page 8

studio
pages 6, 10

chisel
page 9

knives
page 9

photographer
page 18

vase
page 19

clay
pages 9, 16

mural
page 11

sculptor
page 16

wood
page 16

23

Note to Parents and Teachers

Reading for information is an important part of a child's literacy development. Learning begins with a question about something. Help children think of themselves as investigators and researchers by encouraging their questions about the world around them. Each chapter in this book begins with a question. Read the question together. Look at the pictures. Talk about what you think the answer might be. Then read the text to find out if your predictions were correct. Think of other questions you could ask about the topic, and discuss where you might find the answers. Assist children in using the picture glossary and the index to practice new vocabulary and research skills.

Index

Answers to quiz on page 22

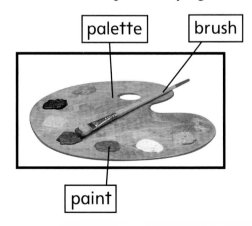

palette brush

paint